Bipolar Dis

MW01295804

and strategies on how you can cope,

manage, and bring back normalcy to your

live after your diagnosis

By: Ken Fisher

Table of Contents

My story

You might be wondering why I am choosing to share my story about Bipolar Disorder. Well, the truth is, I have been through the ups and downs with this mental illness for almost 30 years. My journey has taught me a lot and I feel that by sharing what this "animal" has done to me and the ways in which I have been able to cope, will not only enlighten you but also encourage those of you who are struggling with the same disease as myself. I am 38 years old. I do not take medications anymore! Why? Well, the reason for this is preference. I prefer engaging myself in exercises, nutritional supplements, and therapy to help through managing my condition.

Mania is the most awesome and exciting part of my condition. Yes, it is amazing because I often feel that my energy levels are high and I do not want this stop! The best part of this is the fact that I feel so enthusiastic and optimistic about what I do. You could actually burn down my house and I will respond *"What a great time to explore new home designs and build*!" The main reason for this is that I am most happy and creative during this time. I ensure that I use this time wisely to capitalize on something useful and beneficial to me.

Back in my childhood years, I used to run around and entertain my family and friends. They would laugh at my actions because I was fun. I could simply get lost in the fun and the satisfaction this brought me through the laughs and smiles that I put on their faces. I felt invincible! My mornings during those times were awesome. Now, I simply wake up and get ready for the activities that lie ahead of me despite the fact that sometimes I do not get sufficient sleep. I get everything done on my to-do list and this makes me happy. I Am all over the place engaging in every conversation and domineering in all of them! My family, therapist, and friends often say that I talk too much, too fast and switch from one topic to another making it quite challenging for them to keep up with my awesome pace!

The most unfortunate thing about this time is the fact that I indulge in too much spending and drinking. Actually, I have been in a number of fist fights but not because of anger really. It is because of the exhilarating feeling I get whenever I get into a fight with gigantic guys who are twice or three times bigger than I am. I know that it is indeed dangerous, but all I can think of at the time is that it is entertaining. It is more like a game to me. The upside to this tho is that I have a great sex drive and it is amazing to crave sex. However, this sometimes takes a toll on my relationship because it can be too much for my spouse.

The truth is, during mania, I often feel like I am riding on cloud nine and that my self-worth is way over the top. I cannot really explain this feeling but all I know is that when it burns out, I feel empty. Honestly, without these highs associated with mania, I really do not think I would be able to tolerate the lows that come with depression.

Now comes depression. This is the time when I feel that I should be in this world alone! Not that I want to be by myself forever, but people should just disappear into the thin air. It is more like irrespective of the things I do, people will always be on my neck telling me of all the negative things I have done. Distancing myself then becomes the easiest thing to do.

However, whenever I see people enjoying their lives and having fun, it often reminds me that I am a mental case and the fact that I will never attain that kind of mood stability they so much enjoy. The worst thing during this time is watching and listening to people throwing in their judgments and comparing my mania and depression at times. They often treat me like I am non-existent but desire that their clown comes back from depression to entertain them.

The reason why I choose to dissociate myself at this time is the fact that, to me, they are very annoying. My mindset at this time is negative and this causes me to dread doing anything at all. I actually turn into a grumpy old man. I have even contemplated suicide and have attempted it once. However, the more knowledge I gain about my condition over the years, the more I have gathered that depression is only temporary. It is this self-reminder that has helped me navigate through changes in bipolar disorder episodes and thus, it helps me to avoid doing stupid things and entertain stupid thoughts.

When I am in the middle of depression and mania, it is more like a real world for me. I imagine that this is exactly what "normal" people experience every day. I simply arise from bed in the mornings and suddenly, I feel that everything is fine. I do not panic at some problems, neither do I feel like a clown running around making people laugh at the silly little things I do. I often wish that I could forever maintain this mindset, but I know it is only a wish! I have come to accept that my mood will always change on its own.

Introduction

Bipolar disorder often refers to as a serious mental illness that is characterized by unusual changes in a person's moods. This means that when one is suffering from this illness, they often go from a state of being very happy and active to a very sad, hopeless, down and inactive mood. In between the highs and the lows of their moods, the patient often experiences normal moods. It is the high moods that are clinically referred to as mania and the lows referred to as depression. The causes of Bipolar disorder is often not known. However, what is known is that the disease is genetic and therefore, runs in families. In other cases, research indicates that the potential cause of the disease is an abnormal brain structure and function.

The onset of the Bipolar disorder often begins to occur in a person's late teen years or during their early adulthood. However, I must emphasize that in some cases, research indicates that children, like adults, may have bipolar disorder too. The sad thing about this disease is the fact that it often lasts a lifetime. This is the main reason why most people who have been diagnosed with bipolar disorder are often advised to seek advice from healthcare providers as soon as possible. This is because, when you have a medical checkup, the chance that the doctor will rule out other illnesses associated with mood swings is high, leaving the correct diagnosis that can be managed accordingly.

In cases where the illness is not treated, there is a high chance that it can result in the wreckage of your relationships, careers as well as performances in school. Even worse, the condition may result in the patient committing suicide. In as much as many studies have not come up with a definitive and specific treatment for the illness, there are various treatment methods that have been used in the past and are currently being used in controlling the symptoms of bipolar disorder. Some of these include; talk therapy, medicine, self-help among others.

One thing that is important to note in this case is that Bipolar disorder is not similar to the usual ups and downs that most people experience. Rather, the changes in moods that the patient experience is more extreme. In some cases, these changes are often accompanied by a shift in sleep patterns, levels of energy and the ability to reason in a clearer manner. This means that this illness is so serious to the extent that it has the ability to ruin relationships and thus making it quite challenging for the patient to pursue their career goals or even attend school. The main reason for this is the fact that the changes in moods often can pose a danger to the people in their surrounding or even be detrimental to their own safety.

The good thing about this condition is the fact that when they seek help, they have the chance and the ability to lead a successful life. There are four major types of bipolar disorders, all of which are characterized by changes in moods, activity and energy levels. These types include;

Bipolar I Disorder

This is one of the conditions that is defined by manic episodes which often last up to 7 days. They are also accompanied by manic symptoms that are very severe, and thus, the patient might find the need to seek medical care. In some cases, there is the occurrence of depression that can last up to 14 days. In other cases, depression and manic symptoms may occur together.

Bipolar II Disorder

This is often referred to as a pattern of depression episodes as well as hypomanic episodes. However, it is important to note that it is not the full-blown manic episodes as it is with the Bipolar I disorder.

Cyclothymic Disorder

This is also referred to as cyclothymia. It is often defined by increased number of hypomanic episodes as well as depressive episodes. This often lasts for approximately two years in adults. However, the occurrence and manifestation of these symptoms in children and adolescents last for approximately one year. One important thing to bear in mind, in this case, is that these symptoms are often insufficient for a concrete diagnosis to be made on hypomanic and depressive episodes.

Other specified and unspecified Bipolar and related disorders

These are conditions that are often manifested or defined by bipolar disorder symptoms that do not match those manifested in the above three types of bipolar disorders.

Chapter One: Recognition

Depression just like mania is a very painful experience. This is because, in these states, the person knows that something is amiss. In most cases, most of these feelings are accompanied by anxiety and often gets so intense for the person, to the point where they may leave someone in a state of awe, wondering where they went wrong. In some cases, it is the feelings of extreme fatigue and anxiety that serves as the prime symptom of bipolar disorder.

Signs and symptoms of Depressed state of Bipolar disorder

Some of the major signs of someone that is in a depressed state of bipolar disorder is that in most cases, they experience persistent sadness, emptiness, and anxiety. They often lose interest in many things such as food, sexual activity, and work among others. Despite the fact that the person might have taken adequate rest, they often feel exhausted and fatigued. Sometimes, when they try to sleep, it becomes very challenging and when they do, they often awake too early or even oversleep. Persons with depression often suffer from abnormally with reduced or increased appetite that eventually affects their weight. They often cannot concentrate on what they are doing for long and thus when it comes to making decisions about their work, they are indecisive. This then stimulates feelings of guilt and regret which impairs their sense of self-esteem. It is this low self-esteem that often drives them to have suicidal thoughts.

On the other hand, when it comes to mania or the less intense form of mania, referred to as hypomania, it often is less apparent to the person who is ailing from the disorder. This is because it is often associated with intense feelings of pleasure. The good thing about mania is the fact that they often do not go undiagnosed for extended periods of time. This is because its symptoms are very evident. Some of these symptoms include restlessness, incessancy in their pursuits, over-talkative and insomnia. It is these symptoms that often makes the people in their surroundings feel as if the person is acting out of character.

However, in the case of hypomania where the person is less elated, this might go undiagnosed for extended periods of time. This is because in most cases, this phase is often termed as uncharacteristic for the person. In most cases, if family members are keen, they might have recognized some episodes when the person is experiencing little mild highs. This is because their mood often is unusually buoyant and optimistic.

Signs and symptoms of Mania/Elation in Bipolar disorder

In most cases when the patient is suffering from mania, there is a characteristic alteration in the levels of their feelings that often affects the manner in which they think in an excessive way.

They often feel so high as though they are at the top of the world, better than ever or way better than normal. However, some days, they may be touchy and irritable. They often experience a strong whim of energy that drives them to do a lot of work without taking rest. They may sometimes feel overly active, distractible and restless. This is characterized by great pressure in the head such that their minds cannot be easily switched off.

When they communicate in this state, they often juggle from one topic to another. They demonstrate some unrealistic beliefs in their abilities and this often causes them to have poor judgment in their decision-making process. Unlike someone with depression, persons with mania often have an unrealistically high interest in pleasurable activities. Some of these activities include sexual intercourse, alcohol, new ventures, illegal/street drugs, music, religion, and art among others. While at it, they are normally very demanding, insistent, pushy and exhibit a very proactive behavior. In this state, they cannot see the need for change as they often think that there is nothing wrong with them.

Is Bipolar Disorder more than a mood swing?

Did you know that Bipolar disorder is more than a mood swing? Well, one important thing that you have to take note of is the fact that bipolar disorder is a treatable medical illness. As mentioned earlier, the moods of an individual that is suffering from this illness often span from mania to depression and vice versa. It is these changes in moods that often last for a duration of hours to days, weeks and sometimes even months.

Bipolar disorder affects over two million adults, especially in the United States. Just like other mental conditions such as depression, this often has a great impact on spouses, family members, colleagues at the workplace as well as friends. This illness is not gendered specific, and thus, this is the reason why there is an equal number of men and women that are affected by the disease. It is also prevalent in all ethnic groups, races, ages as well as a social class of people.

People often confuse bipolar disorder and depression. The truth is, based on research, there is evidence that points at a marked difference between bipolar disorders and clinical depression. This is due to the fact that the symptoms and manifestations of the two conditions are similar especially in the depressive episode/phase of bipolar disorder. The mood swings associated with the disorder often span from extreme energy levels to deep despair. It is these extreme changes in the moods that cause a significant disruption of normal activities and thus distinguishing the illness from ordinary changes in the mood.

As opposed to people who suffer from clinical depression, most of the patients who have been diagnosed with bipolar disorder often experience highs and lows of the illness. The highs are what is referred to as mania/euphoria while the lows are often referred to as depression. Under certain climatic conditions such as, during winter and fall, reports indicated that most of the bipolar disorder patients often experience symptoms of depression. However, during the spring, most of them experience symptoms of mania or a less severe form of mania referred to as hypomania.

So what are the complications of bipolar disorder?

Patients with bipolar disorder often have a tough lifestyle which is the result of their behaviors and personalities. In most cases, they have a difficult social life and is often characterized as the culprit for creating family disruptions. This often is a result of someone in an elated state being so domineering, persistent, aggressive, and demanding. These family disruptions may end up in marital breakdowns. Sometimes the person may have behaviors of overspending, increased sexual desire that drives them into extra marital affairs, abusive and aggressive behaviors among others. This in most cases is too much for their spouses to handle and they opt for marital separation, despite several years of a stable marriage.

Other impacts may include, poor work and school performances, loss of employment because of decreased productivity while at work or even worse, abuse of their colleagues causing an unsafe working environment for others. Because of their ability to overspend, they often clean out their bank accounts and may even end up in bankruptcy. Additionally, they may engage in alcohol and illegal substance abuse. This often may lead them to experience legal challenges, sometimes ranging from indiscreet and aggressive behaviors to making illegal remarks, violating traffic rules among other mannerisms that are associated with their overestimation of one's abilities. Because of their extreme behaviors, people often get tired of them, so they may sometimes become isolated. Their isolation from a social life will then contribute to their intense feeling of self-worthlessness, guilt, and depression. It is this loss of self-esteem that finally drives them into a dysphoric manic predicament and create suicidal thoughts.

Types of Bipolar disorder Episodes

Manic episodes: This is often considered as a distinct period of persistent mood elevation. The mood, in this case, is mostly expansive and irritable and lasts for at least a week. An important thing to note is that during manic episodes, three or more symptoms of mania are normally manifested.

Hypomanic episodes: This is quite similar to the manic episodes except for the fact that in this case, the patient does not experience hallucinations or delusions. In other words, the hypomanic episodes are often less severe than the manic episodes, and the patient is not suffering from the typical non-depressed mood. This is because the patient often loses function and thus manifest certain observable behaviors that are out of character.

Major depressive episodes: In this case, most people often experience this for a period of two or more weeks. During this period, the patient is experiencing more than five depression symptoms.

Mixed episodes: This is often the case when the patient is experiencing symptoms of both mania and depression every single day for over a week.

Rapid cycling: This is the period of time during which the patient is experiencing more than four symptoms of mania, hypomania, mixed depression and depression all together for an extended period of up to one year.

Chapter Two: So what really causes Bipolar Disorder?

Based on scientific research, there is a large amount of evidence and reports that point at the occurrence of bipolar disorder as a result of an imbalance in the brain chemicals referred to as neurotransmitters. Despite the fact that the direct cause or etiology of the disease is not very clear, it is well known that environmental, biochemical as well as genetic factors play a role in the causation of the illness. It is important to note that body chemistry in most cases has been attributed to stimulating depression or manic episodes in patients with bipolar disorder. This can also occur due to the presence of other illnesses, hormonal imbalances, stress, and drug abuse as well as altered health habits among others. Additionally, research indicates that bipolar illness is often hereditary and thus runs in the family. Therefore, certain stressful experiences may act as triggers and activate the symptoms of bipolar disorder.

Why it is important to recognize mania

This is something that is very important for you to understand. One thing that most people ignore is treating bipolar disorders. You have to realize that not treating Mania can often open doors to life-threatening situations. Let us examine the case of a woman called Agnes who suffered from mania and was involved in a car accident. Agnes was driving at very high speed because, in her mind, she was a race car driver. On the other hand, a man who had mania invested all his life savings in stock market impulsively and unfortunately lost it all. These are just a few examples of the many people out there suffering from bipolar disorder. In most cases, these behaviors differ from one person to another, but the typical thing is that they are all untreated cases.

Bear in mind that erratic behaviors in itself do not necessarily point to being bipolar. However, if these symptoms or behaviors are recurrent for over a week or more, it is important that you seek medical help from a professional so that you can get an immediate evaluation. The most unfortunate thing is that most people often delay for an extended period of time before they seek treatment or professional help. For bipolar disorder, the average range between the onset of the disease and the correct diagnosis is ten years. This indicates that for as long as the disease is not yet diagnosed, untreated or even undertreated there is a real danger associated with this. This is because, based on research, there are over 20 % cases of suicides reported among bipolar patients who do not receive proper help.

Bipolar disorder in the family line

Despite the fact that the main cause of Bipolar disorder is not yet known, several medical reports and research indicate that the illness is hereditary. According to statistics, there is evidence that demonstrates that 2/3 of people who suffer from bipolar disorder have at least a relative that is suffering from the same illness or unipolar major depression. This is a clear indication that bipolar disorder is genetic and runs in the family.

While bipolar disorders may be considered a hereditary illness, there is not a single way of predicting the manner in which it will affect the other members of the family. This means that if you have such an indication and concern in your family, the most important thing that you have to do is seek the help of a physician. This way, you will have all the questions about symptoms answered and screening for mood disorder performed during the annual medical check-ups. According to DBSA, it is advisable to conduct a thorough screening of all the individuals' health regimen irrespective of whether there is a history of bipolar disorder running in the family or not.

Bipolar disorder in children

It is quite alarming when you recognize the lack of research concerning the onset of bipolar disorder during childhood. The sad thing is that children as young as three years of age have been diagnosed to have the illness and many more children have been shown to exhibit the symptoms of bipolar disorder. More importantly, the symptoms of this illness can be manifested at early infancy. According to research, mothers who have children with bipolar disorder have testified to their children having difficult behaviors and had erratic sleep patterns. In some cases, the children seemed clingy out of the ordinary. Additionally, bipolar children were shown to be uncontrollable, exhibit seizures, tantrums and extraordinary rage from a very young age. In some cases, telling them "no" to something of interest to them would exacerbate their rage.

Similarly, in the case of clinical depression, the first thing that parents have to understand is that whenever they suspect their child of having bipolar disorder, they should immediately seek medical attention for a precise diagnosis. Early and accurate diagnosis of bipolar disorder in children translate to early treatment and thus playing a significant role in the development of the child especially if he or she has a mood disorder.

Chapter Three: Treatment

It is understandable that in some cases, it might be challenging for some people to seek help. If you or someone close to you have a mood disorder, the truth is, you might be feeling a little vulnerable. Therefore, talking to someone about what you are going through is the last thing you would want to do. However, while all these are true, one important thing that you may want to consider, is that finding the correct treatment is often the very first step to becoming an active manager of such an illness as bipolar disorder. This simply means, that for you to find the right treatment, you will first need to find the right mental health professional that will guide you through the process for you to be able to accept, manage and endure all the things that are associated with bipolar disorder.

Choosing a doctor

When you visit a doctor to seek help for your disorder, they may be able to treat the disorder or refer you to a mental health professional who can help. However, under situations where you do not have a family physician that can refer you to a mental health professional, you can turn to your friends, relatives, colleagues that you trust or even members of your support group who may know someone. Additionally, you can simply contact your insurance company or a community mental health center near you who can identify health care providers for you.

Once you have identified a doctor, the first step to recovery is ensuring that you develop trust in the skills, knowledge, and expertise of your doctor. This is simply trusting that they are interested in nothing other than helping you towards recovery. It is important for you to understand that you have nothing to be intimidated about with your doctor. You are not wasting his or her time because that is their job! However, in case you feel that you are not comfortable in any way with your doctor, the first thing is to seek a second opinion from another doctor or even consider changing doctors. You will realize that we are referring to them as doctors instead of therapists, so you can use whatever term you like to refer to the mental practitioner attending to your needs. If you and your healthcare provider decide on what course of treatment is best for your condition, you have to pay attention to the prescriptions made and know that only the medical doctor can make that prescription for you.

Most of your concerns will be addressed by a skilled doctor. This means that when you are seeing your doctor, it is important that you let them know of all the concerns that you have and have them answer all your questions and concerns in a way for you to easily comprehend. Sometimes, while you are at home or in the office, you have all the questions that you would like the doctor to address. The most important thing to do is to write them down before the visit. Do not in any way whatsoever be embarrassed to bring up any subject that does concern your illness. In fact, if it makes you feel much more relaxed, you can tag along with a friend or spouse. Additionally, you can choose to ask the questions in the doctor's office rather than in the examining room if it makes you uncomfortable.

Some of the questions that you might find necessary to ask your mental health practitioner may include;

- The dosage of medication that you are required to take, the time of day or the way in which you can increase the dosage prior to the next visit if necessary. In this case, ensure that you take notes on what the doctor is advising you to do.

- The possible side effects of the medication that the doctor prescribes. This might also include such concerns as the things that you should do in case you experience any side effects. If there are any printed materials saying that the doctor might have to answer this part, ask for it and take it with you to refer in case you are not sure.

- The means through which the patient will be able to reach their doctor or mental health provider in case the condition gets worse with time or in the case of an emergency. This means, that as a patient, the most important thing that you have to remember before exiting the doctor's office is their emergency phone numbers. This will be very instrumental in contacting them in case an emergency arises.

- How you can identify the various signs and symptoms of a particular episode. This information is very important in ensuring that you are not only aware of what you are going through but also have the skills or information on how to respond to them. For instance, if you are experiencing sleepiness, then you know that this has the potential of triggering mania. Therefore, when you feel unusual sleepiness, then you treat it as a new symptom that you can bring it up for discussion with your mental health professional.

- The duration of time it takes for the patient to feel signs of improvement in their conditions. This enables the patient to recognize the type of improvement they anticipate and when they experience it.

- Risks that are associated with the various methods of treatment and the manner through which one can recognize them. This means that, in case you have any concerns about the risks, then you are in a better position to share with your doctor and get the help that is desired.

- The duration through which the patient is expected to take their medications. This is usually very important because once the duration necessary for improvement is reached, and there is no change, then it might be necessary to discontinue the medication.

- The intervals that you need to see your doctor and the time that each appointment lasts. This is important in ensuring that you are better informed on the relevance of seeking medical advice and you can be able to plan accordingly depending on your schedule and what works best for you. Additionally, sometimes, the appointment might include seeking psychotherapy and the type that is recommended.

- The other important thing that you need to check is whether there is anything that you can do to improve your condition. These can also include activities that you have to avoid in order to increase your chances of improvement. Additionally, if the medication that you are taking currently is not very effective, then inquire from your doctor whether there are alternative treatments and what they are. This means that if someone were to question the medication that your mental health professional recommended or even worse raise doubts concerning the possible dangers that the treatment poses to the patient, you should be in a better position to give a response.

Medications

One thing that I often tell myself when it comes to taking medications is "*I do not want to rely on pills to solve my problems*" In the same manner, I am certain that many of you might have had a similar reaction when you were told you are suffering from a mood disorder. How can a pill help me recover from an attitude related disorder? Why can't they just teach us how to be happy in life? These are some of the questions that crossed my mind from the very first time medication for my disorder was recommended to me.

However, in as much as things might not be clear to you at the very beginning, you have to bear in mind that bipolar disorder like depression often affects the normal functioning of the brain. This means that you are not going through those experiences and symptoms because you are a bad person or lacking in something in any way. Let me ask you "would you consider someone suffering from diabetes to be lacking just because they have insufficient insulin to regulate their blood sugar levels? Would you blame them for feeling nervous and tired at times because of their condition?" Well, the truth of the matter is that the choice to take medications for your condition solely depends on you. However, whatever choice you make, you have to bear in mind that many people who suffer from bipolar disorder like you and I do, have taken medications and their conditions have improved tremendously.

This choice is the very reason why so many patients have saved their lives from pain, agony, and self-destruction that is associated with untreated bipolar disorder. Despite the fact that medication does not promise to solve all the problems that you might be having, the right intake of the drugs can improve your ability to cope with the problems that are associated with the condition. The reward of this is an improvement in health and restoration in your sense of judgment.

According to a report released by the Food and Drug Administration (FDA), there are several numbers of drugs that have received approval for use in the treatment of mood disorders. These medications are often classified into various categories based on the distinct chemical structure it has. It is the role of this chemical structure to target various brain receptors and thus offering a wide range of benefits. Though many of us might be diagnosed with bipolar disorder, we are all very different from each other. It is this individual difference that has contributed to DBSA not placing a preference or recommendation for any particular treatment over the other.

However, bear in mind that taking these drugs does not guarantee that they will work the same way for everyone. This is the main reason why you have to ensure that you consult with your doctor before you take any prescription. You have to be aware of what you are taking, the reason why you are taking it and for how long you will be taking the drugs. Additionally, you have to be aware of the side effects of the medications you are taking and if the drugs have synergistic effects with other prescriptions drugs, drugs bought over the counter or any supplements that you might be taking. Always remember that you are entitled to as many answers as possible to all the concerns and questions that you might have to ensure that you are comfortable with the medication that the doctor puts you on.

So what then do you expect while taking medication?

In most cases, medications are prescribed with the main aim of relieving the symptoms of a given condition you might be experiencing. You do not have to be experiencing all the symptoms indicated in this book for you to be certain that you are suffering from bipolar disorder. Therefore, you will need to work hand in hand with your doctor in creating the best strategy that has the highest possibility of easing the symptoms that you are experiencing.

With bipolar disorder, symptoms associated with depression and mania are often stabilized by taking mood stabilizers. These can take up to two weeks in order to gain the full effect. Sometimes, your doctor might want to fine tune your treatment by either increasing or reducing your dosage depending on what they discovered from their evaluation. Additionally, sometimes the doctor might find it necessary to add you another medication to your treatment course based on what symptoms you are experiencing. For instance, you might find that a mood stabilizer is prescribed together with antipsychotic drugs or antidepressants.

Despite the fact that there have been so many reports refuting the ingestion of all the drug combinations I have mentioned in the paragraph above, you have to understand that medications which are used in the treatment of mood disorders are not addictive and do not have the ability to alter your personality, even if you experience the feeling of withdrawal whenever you are off medications. Whatever you do, ensure that you do not stop taking your medications without informing your doctor first.

Mood stabilizers

The main goal of treating a patient with bipolar disorder with mood stabilizers is to ensure that their mood is kept within normal range. While there are so many experts who agree that mood stabilizers are the best medications for this mental illness, the term is not really a scientific one. Some of the most common ones that most experts agree upon include lithium, valproate, olanzapine, lamotrigine and carbamazepine among others. Each one of these drugs I have mentioned has been shown to be effective in treating mania as well as in prevention of relapses. Of all these mood stabilizers mentioned, Olanzapine is one of the drugs that research has demonstrated to having excellent benefits in the treatment of acute mania. Additionally, it has antidepressant benefits and thus appears to be very effective in preventing manic relapses.

An important point to note is that when you refer to a drug as a mood stabilizer, it has to possess certain characteristics. Some of these properties include working as a treatment for mania, depression, and relapses. It also has to have the ability not to increase the mood cycling rate of the patient or even cause a sudden switch from one abnormal mood state to another. Other medications that mood experts often prescribe their patients include Calan, Isoptin, Omega-3 fatty acids and Trileptal among others. However, these drugs are still categorized under the class of drugs that have not yet been proven. This is because none of them has scientific data on its use in a rigorous study nor do they have any approvals by FDA for the treatment of mental illnesses such as bipolar disorder.

An important thing that you should bear in mind is that all medications do have side effects. The main aim is for you as a bipolar disorder patient to work closely with your doctor to ensure that you find a mood stabilizer that works best for you. By this I mean, the medication has to have the ability to ease or prevent episodes of mania and depression without causing adverse side effects that will further impair your health.

Antidepressants

There is a wide range of antidepressants which plays a significant role in the treatment of depression episodes in a patient with bipolar disorder. However, bear in mind that their use has to be closely monitored by a health professional. The main reason for this is, based on previous research, there is an indication that certain patients often transition from depression to mania whenever they are treated using antidepressant medications. This means, in spite the usefulness of antidepressants in the treatment of depression, they often can cause an overshoot from normal mood to mania. Conversely, some of the patients with bipolar disorder who are on anti-depressants may not experience this impulsive switch in mood, rather, they often suffer from worsening cases of their depressive episodes of bipolar disorder. For this particular reason, it is important that each patient ensures that they have regular communication with their medical professional. These follow-ups play a significant role in ensuring that the medications the doctor has put you on are not making your condition worse. It is the role of your physician to ensure that they monitor you for any manic symptoms. In as much as the doctor has a role to play here, it is important that your family, friends and trusted loved ones offer their assistance as you go through treatment.

It is always highly and vitally important for you to be clear, concise and honest with your doctor concerning what you are feeling. This means that, whenever you notice feelings of lack of sleep, restlessness, racing thoughts, excessive speech or even hyperirritability during the process of taking your antidepressant medications, the first step here is to report these symptoms to your doctor with immediate effect.

Despite the fact that a low level of mood elevation may be desirable and brings a little pleasure, the truth is, it can be extremely frightening when they escalate into mania. Remember that mania is one of the disorders which causes major problems in your life. This means, that for you to keep control of your life and focus on the goals that you want to achieve, you must report any symptoms as soon as you notice them, as time is of extreme importance at this point and should be treated as such.

Therefore, when you keep a close watch on your condition, you are simply creating a recipe for effectively treating your bipolar depression.

Antipsychotics

This refers to the drugs that were initially designed for the treatment of hallucinations and delusions that are often caused by a condition referred to as schizophrenia. However, over the years, research indicate that antipsychotic medications often have anti-manic effects even in bipolar patients with mania, despite the fact that they do not suffer from psychosis. This means that their prescription is often done whenever a patient is experiencing manic episodes. Ingestion of these drugs plays a significant role in ensuring that it clears up distortions and disorganization in thinking as well as hallucinations.

One of the most common properties of antipsychotic drugs is their ability to block the receptors of these molecules or neurotransmitters referred to as dopamine. The release of too many dopamines in the brain is the major contributing factor to the occurrence of mania. This is the reason why most doctors or physicians refer to this as a neuroleptic. Some of the older drugs that were used as powerful blockers of dopamine include Thorazine, Haldol, Prolixin, Navane, and Mellaril among others.

As a class of bipolar disorder medications, neuroleptics often play a significant role in the treatment of acute mania. However, they often result in side effects that are adverse and thus, limiting their usefulness. During early times of treatment, patients treated with neuroleptics often experience stiffness of the muscles, restlessness, and tremors. In the long term, the impact of these neuroleptics on the patient is potentially irresistible movement disorder. Some of these disorders include tardive dyskinesia. This is a disorder that is characterized by involuntary movements that occur without purpose and they keep recurring over and over.

Today, there are new antipsychotic drugs that are available in the market for treatment of mania. The first one was referred to as Clozapine which is often called atypical antipsychotic medication. Some other members of the new class of antipsychotic medications include risperidone, ziprasidone, quetiapine, aripiprazole, and olanzapine among others. Just like the older drugs that I mentioned above, the newer class of antipsychotic drugs have the ability to block dopamine receptors. However, it does this with less potency than the older drugs. Additionally, the Clozapine has the ability to block serotonin. It is such drugs that have dopamine blockade and serotonin blockade that have a lesser likelihood of causing side effects that are intolerable. For treatment of acute mania, they are often used in combination with mood stabilizers.

Once the patient recovers from manic episodes, it is recommended that the patient lowers their dosage of antipsychotic medications as a standard practice. However, the most unfortunate thing for some patients is the fact that once they lower the dosage, they begin to experience manic symptoms more severely. For this particular group of patients, the use of antipsychotic drugs is prescribed continuously to prevent reoccurrence of mania. As a result, antipsychotic drugs may be thought of as a treatment for both mania and prevention of psychotic symptoms.

Anxiolytic

These drugs are often referred to as anti-anxiety medications. Anxiety is one of the problems that often is associated with episodes of mania and depression in patients diagnosed with bipolar disorder. One of the most frequently used medications in this class is referred to as benzodiazepines. Some of these medications include Valium, Xanax, Ativan and Klonopin among others. These drugs are useful in the treatment of sleeplessness and anxiety symptoms of bipolar disorder. The intake of these benzodiazepines is very significant in controlling the symptoms that appear during early cases of hypomania. However, benzodiazepines potentially lead to addiction or physical and psychological overdependence.

The intake of such drugs is often associated with high chances of abuse. This is the reason why it sometimes causes a rapid effect that is quickly rid of from the blood stream. Some of the examples in this class include alprazolam also referred to as Xanax. The potential for abuse of these drugs is lower because they often have a slower effect and take a longer time in the bloodstream. Most standard antidepressants often have an excellent effect when it comes to the reduction of anxiety. However, the thing is that they require a longer duration of several weeks of consistent use for it to be effective. As a result, it may lead to worse situations of bipolar disorder in some patients.

Alternative treatment

According to DBSA, there are several medications that get into the marketplace and claim to have a positive effect on bipolar disorder. Some of these medications include Omega-3, SAM-e, and St. John's wort among others. In spite the fact that these drugs are being sold in the marketplace, an important thing that you have to bear in mind is that DBSA does not endorse or discourage the intake of these drugs for the treatment of bipolar disorder. The main reason for this kind of indifference is the fact that there is a lack of scientific evidence to support the action of these drugs. This means that you should remain vigilant about such medications. This is because while some drugs might want to claim their positive effects hiding behind those being natural products, this does not always translate into them being safe. On the other hand, there is a wide range of supplements that are present in the marketplace. The difference between them is that they contain different quantities of the active ingredient and they may have adverse side effects or even worse synergistic interactions with prescribed medication, and hence, interfering with their efficiency in treatment. Therefore, always pay attention to not only what has been written on labels medications but also discuss with your doctor or pharmacist about these drugs before you take them.

The most important thing when it comes to medications is ensuring that what you are taking have concrete clinical research evidence of their efficiency and safety. It is also paramount that before you take any prescription, you have consulted or discussed it with your medical practitioner before taking the treatment or even modify it.

Electroconvulsive Therapy (ECT)

This is the kind of treatment method that is often recommended for treatment of people with severe depression and mania. In most cases, this treatment method is used when psychotherapy fails to adequately cause a significant reduction in the symptoms of bipolar disorder. This is the point where the ECT is considered to be safe and effective as an alternative treatment method. An important thing to note about this method of treatment is that you cannot force it on people or even use it as a form of submission.

The mode of action of this treatment method is through mild electrical stimulation of the brain. This causes seizures that in turn often causes relief of depression. In this case, the patient is often given mild anesthetics to eliminate shaking. Therefore, an average of about twelve treatments is often administered to the patient within a duration of 3-4 weeks. Once the treatment is a success, subsequent episodes of depression are often managed using antidepressants or less frequent doses of ECT.

Just like all the other treatments, ECT has the potential to cause side effects. Despite the fact that most bipolar disorder patients that have been treated using ECT say that this method has disturbances on their memory, they claim that the benefits that come with this technique often outweighs the long-term effects of severe, painful unremitting depression. This is often the case when it comes to patients who are suicidal. This is because they would have otherwise hidden their impulses had they waited for their medication to take effect.

Light Therapy

Did you know that full spectrum light is the light that contains all the wavelengths of natural sunlight? Did you know that the absence of full spectrum light has the possibility of causing Seasonal Affective Disorder (SAD)? This is essentially a form of depression that develops typically during fall and winter and lasts through late spring and summer. According to research findings, there is evidence that indicates mild to moderate cases of SAD can be effectively treated using light therapy.

The mode of action of this treatment method often involves the process of exposing the patient to a type of full spectrum light that essentially compensates for the loss of daylight. Therefore, if this is your preferred method of treating your bipolar disorder, you have to ensure that you check with your doctor about what type of light would be ideal for treating your condition.

Psychotherapy

This is also referred to as talk therapy. It often serves as the most important part of bipolar disorder treatment for many people. In cases where the patient is suffering from mild to moderate depression, you will find that this method of treatment is effective when used alone. However, in cases where the patients are suffering from a more severe form of depression, psychotherapy alone may not be beneficial. This means that the patient has to undergo a different form of treatment in order to relieve them of their symptoms.

When you are suffering from bipolar disorder or chronic cases of depression, it is important that you use talk therapy in combination with medication. With the help of a good therapist, you can be successful in modifying your behavior and emotional patterns that often contribute to your illness. Several types of psychotherapy are present. Such include; cognitive-behavioral, interpersonal, family, marriage, and group therapies among others. Therefore, it is highly important to take into consideration a thorough research to determine which one of the above methods would be most effective for you. Always remember that even though you are seeing a psychotherapist, you still need to always consult with your doctor. This is because, in spite of the fact that psychotherapists are highly trained medical professionals, they are not medical doctors and thus, you cannot take medication prescription from them.

Hospitalization

There are a wide range of reasons why a doctor or a physician will recommend that a patient is hospitalized if they have severe depression or bipolar disorder. Some of the reasons include;

side effects of medications which may have rendered the patient unable to care for him or herself, discontinuity of medications and thus need to monitor and control medication from the hospital or in the case of attempted suicide by the patient. Additionally, the patient may generally require a controlled environment with close supervision by the doctors to monitor their recovery progress and the manner in which they are or are not responding to treatment.

It is important for you to understand that, if hospitalization is a recommendation, then you have to ask questions concerning the treatment course as well as the estimated length of stay. You should ensure that you are certain of what health care provider or insurance company will cover your costs while in the hospital. It is not surprising that most patients do not like being hospitalized. However, it is important to understand that you cannot be hospitalized unless the doctors have assessed your situation and found it necessary. This can be because you do not have the ability to take care of yourself or even worse, you may be a threat to yourself/suicidal and thus must be admitted a hospital whether voluntarily or involuntarily.

Always ensure that you have access to the contacts of the state's attorney office, psychiatrist, police, and home emergency numbers to ensure that you are aware of all the legal procedures required. Remember that despite the fact that you could be admitted involuntarily, it often could prove to be a lifesaver.

Support

Reaching out for help

When I was first diagnosed with a mental illness, the first thing that came over me is fear. I am certain that you felt it too! I went on and on in my head wondering what I should do and ask myself why this happened to me and not anyone else. I kept thinking that something wrong happened to me. It is these questions that often pushed me into allowing fear to get deeper and I felt broken and not worthy of living! It is this fear that I now realize is actually emanated from stigma.

You might be asking yourself, what is a stigma? Well, according to the definition given by the Webster dictionary, stigma refers to a mark of shame, stain or discredit. When you are newly diagnosed, sometimes, it is easy for the community and the people around you to mock, ridicule and laugh at you for the condition that you have and this brings on a stigma. However, one thing that I will tell you for sure is that you will need to manage your mood disorder and also take control of managing the symptoms associated with it. Adjusting to the opinions of the people in and around your surroundings is also of vital importance. You must be able to tell yourself that you have no control over other people's actions, nor their reaction towards you and your condition. We all should know by now that sickness has absolutely no fear of neither gender, race nor class, so, you may have bipolar disorder but the people who chose to ridicule and judge you may already have a disease of some sort lingering in their bodies that is not yet known to them. This kind of mindset will give you the mental strength you will need to cope in those difficult times. Some might refer to you as someone crazy! Do not worry! I know this is easier said than done, but despite the fact that these statements are often devaluing and unacceptable, you should not let them prevent you from seeking the help that you need. My illness does not define who I am and it should be the same for you.

How to take control of your illness

Just as in the case of many other chronic illnesses such as diabetes, asthma, and heart diseases, bipolar disorder is an illness that you can manage by yourself. Despite the fact that bipolar disorder, like depression, is not curable, the good thing is that it can be treated. Allow yourself to see the glass as half full rather than half empty. Allow yourself to have a positive thinking. The truth is that you might have a positive attitude that may motivate you to take the first step and get the treatment that you need. That very initial treatment may be the only medication you will ever need for your illness. By this, I mean that you should shake off the fear that you have allowed into your life and take a chance to wellness and wholeness. Remember! There are many other diseases out there that are so complicated that there isn't even treatment, let alone cure. Be optimistic and practice being your biggest motivator moving forward. More importantly, only allow positive and encouraging people in your circle. Do not be intimidated by negative individuals and do not be afraid to eliminate any form of negativity from your life.

For many people suffering from bipolar disorder and experiencing severe cases of depression or manic episodes, they may have these experiences causing them stigma at certain points in their lives. If this happens, I want to ask you to, BE

OPTIMISTIC! DO NOT BE AFRAID!. Take this as a good thing. This is because, with every experience that you have with previous episodes, you are certain that this places you miles ahead in the process of recognizing the symptoms you have and seeking the necessary help.

Did you know that there are people with bipolar disorder who are treated briefly and they are able to complete their treatment in less than a year? However, for others, daily medications and frequent visits to the mental health professional forms part of their lives. Whichever the category you fall in, always bear in mind that you have to continue your medication. This is the only way you will be able to significantly lower your chances of having recurrent symptoms over time.

Sharing with others about your illness

When I was first diagnosed with bipolar disorder, I was afraid of people knowing that I had the illness. The truth is, each person who have been down this road, are often concerned about people knowing. This is because you are afraid of people looking at you in a different manner, thinking of you as crazy or simply isolating you once they know that you have a mood disorder. In as much as it is your personal choice to reveal your medical condition to the public or anyone else other than your physician, it is important that you share it with the people close to you, who you can confide in, so that you can get some additional support to get through the reality of your diagnosis.

In as much as there are bad people out there who do not understand this mental illness, many people will surely appreciate your illness. By sharing with them, you are simply allowing them to be a part of your journey through conquering the illness. This way, you will not feel like you are left out. Rather, you are helping the people that matter most in your life to understand what you are ailing from and the manner in which they should effectively respond to your mood swings. Additionally, based on the fact that bipolar disorder and side effects of its medication have the ability to cause impairment of the brain function, it is important that you raise this concern with your employer. This is especially critical if your job is concerned with people and thus their safety is at stake.

In as much as disclosing your mental illness may be challenging when you have bipolar disorder, it is important that the employer does not let this out. This is unless the information about the employee's mental state is necessary for demonstrating their eligibility for accommodation under Americans with Disabilities Act (ADA) and only when this accommodation is required. Additionally, the employer might be interested in confidentiality rights under the ADA. Whatever the case, you have to understand that the main interest and the mandate of the company is to ensure that they are able to safeguard your mental health in addition to offering reasonable accommodations. This is because, if the bipolar disorder remains untreated, the danger at the workplace would be absenteeism significant reduction in productivity and occurrence of work-related injuries.

Self-Care

Have you ever thought of the impact of maintaining good health when you are suffering from a mental illness or a chronic disease? Well, the truth is that maintenance of good health habits may not be a cure for bipolar disorder. However, it can have a tremendous effect on your overall sense of wellness. By good health habits, I am simply referring to such things as exercise, good diet, and regular sleep habits among others that play a critical role in helping one to feel better. On the other hand, there are several factors that also hinder improvement from mental health disorders. Some of these include stress, poor sleep habits, other illnesses, food sensitivities, malnutrition and deficiencies, substance abuse, isolation and improper metabolism among others.

In most cases, you will find that many people who have been diagnosed with not only bipolar disorder but other chronic diseases such as diabetes, cancer, heart problems among others, often opt to engage in alcohol and illegal drug abuse. Well, in as much as this can be tempting at times, just so that you can "cope" with stress, they are very harmful habits that will contribute to poor prognosis. This is because when you abuse these substances, you are simply making your condition worse and also contributes to alteration in the effectiveness of medication. Therefore, if you have a difficult time stopping the use of alcohol and illegal drugs in your ill state, you have to take a step further and speak to your healthcare provider, family or a trusted friend to get help.

Another helpful strategy that you can employ is keeping a journal that will simply help you to chart important activities. Such things include exercise, nutrition, menstrual cycle, healthcare updates among others. The main importance of this is to ensure that you have the ability to determine some of the contributing factors to your mood disturbance and mood improvement. This way, you have the ability to avoid engaging in those that make your condition worse and choose to stick by those that promise to improve your health. Once you have your journal chart, it is important that you share it with your healthcare provider so that you get further support and help on how you progress towards recovery.

Suicide prevention

Now that you are reading this book, I assume that you are either suffering from bipolar disorder or you have a friend or loved one with this illness. Well, one of the most important things that you should take note of when you are in this mental state is the urge and drive to commit suicide. If you or your loved one has suicidal thoughts, the first thing that you have to do is to recognize and accept these thoughts for what they are. This is simply you expressing the treatable mental condition. You should not be embarrassed about this. You should not allow these thoughts to get in the way of effective communication with your doctor, friends or family members. The best thing to do is to seek immediate medical attention.

Some of the important steps that you can take in order to ensure that you manage these symptoms are; first speaking to your mental health professional. Additionally, you can choose to speak to a friend or family member that you trust and are not finding it difficult to open up to them. You should also ensure that you schedule regular visits to your doctor. Since this comes with impulsive behaviors, you can instruct one of the people that are close to you to take your credit cards, car keys, checkbooks among other valuables when the thoughts of committing suicide become very persistent. Ensure that in your place of residence is a safe box, you should not have guns, weapons or old medications that may tempt you into committing suicide. Instead, it is advisable that you keep images, pictures or memory books of people you love most close to you.

Develop wellness lifestyle

While you work towards discovering the various ways in which you can minimize the symptoms of bipolar disorder, it is important that you pay close attention to wellness. Some of the simple ways in which you can make this happen are, simply talking to your doctor on a regular basis, call a friend that you confide in and share talking and listening to them and during your free time, you can engage in exercises that will help you to relax, reduce stress and remained focused. One of the ways of keeping active is by taking part in things that you find to be fun, creative and affirming.

Additionally, always keep your journal close to you, so you write down your thoughts and feelings as they present themselves. The best way to keep up with this is by simply keeping a daily planning calendar. In all the things that you engage in, I want you to ensure that you stay away from alcohol and illegal drugs. Allow yourself to get better by changing your mind and renewing your strength through the power of positive thinking! You can do this by first changing your diet, finding a stimulatory surrounding and attending a local DBSA support group that will uplift you and keep you in check on a regular basis.

Family and Friends

When it comes to living with someone with bipolar disorder or depression, the truth is that everyone who has been down this road will admit to it being challenging. This means, when you are a friend with, a family to or a trusted supporter of someone who has bipolar disorder, you have to ensure that you stay up to date about the facts that surround the illness and the manner in which the individual is progressing. The main aim of doing this is to ensure that you are able to come in to help whenever you can and knowing when to leave things as they are. For instance, if your friend with the severe bipolar disorder does not wish to see visitors, the first thing that you have to do is to support their decisions. This is because, forcing them to see visitors when they are not willing to do so, may be like adding salt to an open wound.This may cause a breakdown for them instead of lifting their spirits and their reaction may become one of violence when their levels of anxiety heighten. On the other hand, if your friend or family with bipolar disorder is experiencing serious depression episodes, you should stay close to them. The main reason why this is very advisable is to ensure that they do not pose a threat to self and the people around them especially if they had exhibited suicidal thoughts.

Additionally, when you are with someone who is prone to manic episodes, the first thing that you should do is ensure that you set rules when they are in a stable mood. The main reason for this is to allow you and them to engage in a discussion on how to safeguard them and their behaviors during heightened moods. Such precautions would be confiscating their checkbooks, credit cards, car keys and their banking privileges. As it is, in the case of suicidal depression, a manic patient is often out of control and may endanger their lives and that of others. One of the helpful things that most people do in such a situation is confining them in a hospital at least until the end of their episodes.

Another thing that family is advised to do is to take turns checking in on the bipolar patient. This is because, just like any other patient with a mental illness, it can be overwhelming for a single person. The best way to get over stress and the burden that this mental illness comes with is to focus on other fun activities and events. This is especially the case when there are young children and teenagers in the home. You can explain to them that there is someone in the family with a mental illness. This is to ensure that they offer their support, continued attention and undying love to them. This is very important also in ensuring that the children understand what the mental illness is about and that it is not because the patient did anything wrong to deserve what they are going through.

Once the person has recovered from the symptoms of their illness, it is important that as family and friends, you allow them the space to approach life at their own speed. Try to do things as a family so that you help them to regain their confidence. By forcing them and managing their lives from left right and center, you are simply stripping them of their self-confidence and they might believe that they cannot do anything unless someone is there to push them around. You must always bear in mind that having a mental illness often predisposes one to the vulnerability of losing their self-esteem. This means that it might take a long period of time before they can be able to regain it and become comfortable, whether in school, home, work or when in the company of friends.

It is important that once they recover, you treat them the same way you have always treated them. As you do this, you have to pay attention to the possible recurrence of these episodes and symptoms. The truth is that it is possible for you to notice the symptoms recurring before they can even notice. In a loving and caring manner, the first thing you do is to carefully suggest to them about visiting a mental health professional so that they can get the help that they need as early as possible.

Value of DBSA support groups

As someone who was diagnosed with bipolar disorder early in life, I will tell you that it does suck! However, you do not deserve to be alone. There are so many DBSA support groups where you are able to meet with people who have the same condition as yours. Here, you will not feel ashamed of anything and sharing with these people will be very helpful because they understand what you are going through firsthand. Look around your area and identify a DBSA group that you can comfortably join. The members are people with bipolar disorder as well as some members of families with people suffering from bipolar illness.

An important thing about these groups is the fact that they serve as a complete complement of formal therapy. This is because they often can help in increasing compliance to treatment and thus support their patients to avoid hospitalization. It also plays a critical role in ensuring that they have access to a forum where they can feel accepted and understood. This offers them the chance to discover themselves and the group also allow the patients to be aware of their ability to understand that their bipolar disorder does not define who they are and thus, they can benefit from the experiences that others have been through.

Chapter Four: How to manage Bipolar Disorder

In spite of the fact that there are many ways that one can be able to treat bipolar disorder, the most important thing that we need to recognize is that there is no cure for this kind of mental illness. This means that we only have the ability to manage the illness. The best way to do this is by simply exercising care. The main reason why care is important is the fact that it contributes towards proper diagnosis and acceptance of the illness, it creates an infrastructure that is geared towards providing adequate care and love to the patients, and it definitely contributes towards establishing a better life. Here is an example of the results you will accomplish according to the steps you take, and the factors that actively come into play to attain great livelihood and normalcy living with bipolar disorder.

When it comes to management, these are the various steps that will indicate whether or not you are on the right journey of managing the disorder with a great degree of success. An important thing to note is that the symptoms of bipolar disorder are often spotted with the manifestation of severe crisis in the life of the person. This is the time when the patient has to go through mandatory treatment according to the Mental Health Act, 2007. However, in the case of people with bipolar disorder type 2 and 3, they have the ability to recognize the onset of the symptoms of their illnesses at a very early stage. This is the time when they are able to consult with their doctors and they can be referred to a psychiatrist for accurate diagnosis.

Lack of Insight

One of the setbacks when it comes to people with bipolar disorder is the fact that they have a distinct lack of insight and destructive behaviors. This, in most cases, for patients with mania often cannot be diagnosed early enough because there is a lack of testing. This means that for an accurate diagnosis to be made, it takes several years.

Towards diagnosis

An important thing to take into consideration as a bipolar patient is accepting the diagnosis outcome. This is because, when you choose to remain in denial, you are simply paving the way for recurrent cycles of crisis and re-diagnosis, if you fail to address this situation, it will last for several years and deteriorate with time and poor health habits

Being a patient with bipolar disorder, I can assure you that it is not easy to accept the fact that you have been diagnosed with this condition. The main reason for this is often the stigma that is associated with most mental illnesses. This is despite the tremendous efforts that many organizations and activists have made in the past few decades. Really, would you want to admit to yourself or anyone else that you are a mental case?

Manic depression is really frightening especially during the early stages. This is because in most cases, you do not have any clue what is happening to you. You often feel that you are out of control and have no idea when this might re-occur. The main reason is that you most likely do not have any control over your emotions and feelings and thus act out of impulse. The result of this is suffering for the people that are closest to you such as family and friends. As I mentioned earlier, it is extremely important that you accept the diagnosis and take control over your life. As someone with the illness, there are three milestones that have helped me cope with my illness and thus, effectively manage my condition despite the various challenges that are faced along the journey. These milestones include;

1. *Acceptance*

This is the very first milestone towards managing bipolar disorder. Did you know that illnesses often has the ability to get to the core of your sense of being? Well, this is very true. Mental illness especially has the power to destroy your self-confidence and your self-esteem. This means that if you fail to accept your condition, you are simply marking timing on the same ground and thus, making it much more difficult to move forward. At this very stage, information is very paramount. When you allow yourself to meet people with the similar condition, you are simply allowing them to share their experiences and thus, informing your thought process. Look around your locality, you will not miss a psychiatrist or two who run small groups for people with bipolar disorder. Join them!

2. Insight

Once you have accepted that you are bipolar, the next step is insight. An episode of their mental illness does not just come out of the blues. The truth of the matter is, almost every person has an alarm warning of some kind of illness. In most cases, these warning signals are often personal. However, if you are experiencing mania, this might manifest through irritability, lack of sleep, intense sexual desires among others. In the case of depression, some of the early signals include tiredness, avoiding the company of people as well as losing interest in pleasurable activities such as sex.

In all this, you have to understand that the occurrence of an episode of bipolar disorder is often triggered by a particular problem. This can be career challenges, personal relationships, and stress among others. In both cases of mania and depression, you have to become aware and vigilant of these changes and ensure that you consult the doctor about any possibilities in changing your medications.

3. Action

The final milestone is acting. With insight, you will be able to act out of concrete information and evidence rather than acting out blindly. The first thing, in this case, is to come up with an action plan. This is very critical in ensuring that you have all the practical responses laid out should an episode of bipolar disorder arise. This should be designed in such a way that you can easily follow through whenever you are able to. Additionally, it should have the ability to dictate to the caregivers, family, and close friends, of the effective manner in which they can intervene. Therefore, do not be afraid, rehearse the plan and ensure that you keep it up to date at all times.

Managing your bipolar disorder in an effective manner simply means ensuring that you maintain good mental health between episodes. The best way to achieve this is by ensuring that you keep track of small changes in your mood so that it will be easy for you to determine the early onset of the symptoms. This is very important in ensuring that you can act on it before true depression and mania kicks in. In most cases, mania and depression can be maladaptive responses to aspects of stress. This means that you can use them to ensure that you channel your thoughts somewhere other than problems that you are facing.

When you face problems in life, you develop the ability to sort these problems out and thus, realistically maintain a healthy mental stability. One of the ways in which you can effectively manage bipolar disorder is by ensuring that you perform a regular review of your anxieties and stresses. By doing so, it will enable you to avoid the problems building up and provoking occurrence of a crisis.

In order to achieve this effectively, my advice to you would be to nurture a strong and healthy social network. When you do this, you will soon realize that your close friends, family, and community around you will not be frightened away and thus will serve as valuable tools in giving you helpful feedback to thrust you to the next level of recovery. It is your close relations that will, in most cases, notice that something is not right. Additionally, it is their social support that will go a long way in ensuring that you achieve mental stability and health. Remember, part of staying healthy and whole is taking care of the relationships we have so that we can sail through the turbulence of our illness.

After all, is said and done about managing bipolar disorder, a crucial thing to take note of is that the last two milestones; 'Insight and Action,' have little to do with the treatment of your illness. Rather, it is much more concerned with rebuilding your life once you have adequate mastery and knowledge of the symptoms. It is this knowledge that you have achieved that will not only help you to gain control over potentially damaging impacts of the illness but also help you through the journey towards restoring your self-esteem and confidence.

It is the resulting confidence and self-esteem that will go a long way in helping you to explore novel avenues and life's possibilities. This way, you are simply opening yourself up to new opportunities which will thrust you to new heights that you have always desired and that really is vital to your happiness. You will be surprised at how this plays a critical role in restoring to you; new relationships, interests, security as well as employment/career growth and prosperity.

Stress and Schedule Management

What is the role of stressful situations in Bipolar disorder?

Stressful situations are often triggered by a number of factors. These factors often include things like interpersonal conflicts or financial challenges among others. These factors are attributed to increasing the likelihood of manic and depressive episodes of bipolar disorder. In some cases, life events such as marriage, the pressure at the workplace, shifting jobs among others may be the cause of these episodes. In this chapter, we will discuss the various techniques that you can employ in your treatment. It is important that you select those techniques that you find valuable to improving your condition or that of your loved one.

Managing sleep patterns

Based on research findings, there is a clear indication that alterations in the sleep cycle from normal one often is a trigger to increasing the risks of developing mania of depression. Considering the fact that you cannot always avoid stress, you should ensure that you strive to maintain your normal sleep patterns. The most important thing about this is so that you can be able to maintain a stable mood throughout the day. The best way in which you can employ sleep in buffering against manic and depressive episodes of bipolar disorder is by waking up and retiring to bed at the same time always regardless of whether it is a weekday or a weekend.

Despite the fact that it can be tempting to stay up late or even sleep in during the weekends, any change in your sleep patterns is a recipe for disaster. What I would like you to always remember is that the more consistent you are in the time you wake and go to sleep each day, the more stable your mood will be. You do not have to carry out this strategy in an all-or-nothing manner. Instead, if you find it quite challenging to maintain a regular sleep pattern, it is up to you to select a sleep schedule that is more defined and works best for you especially during stressful periods.

Some of the most important and beneficial sleep tips that you can employ includes the following;

Keeping stress out of the bedroom

When it comes to sleeping, then you should actually exercise sleep. This means that when you get to the bedroom, let it be your number one priority to ensure that you do not discuss any stressful situations concerning your family, job or friends while in the bedroom. Therefore, all you should do is preserve the bedroom for sleep activities only.

Use muscle relaxation techniques while in bed

When you get to bed, you can use relaxation tapes to help enhance your relaxation and thus boost your comfort in bed. Always bear in mind that the goal is not going to sleep. Rather, it is about attaining comfort and relaxation so that sleep is naturally triggered. There are so many commercially available tapes that you can purchase to help you achieve bedtime relaxation.

Do not exert yourself to get to sleep

Whenever you find it difficult to get sleep, refrain from trying too hard! The main reason for this is the fact that when you try too hard to get sleep, you are only causing the opposite effect to take place. This means that you will stay awake and frustrated. The best thing you can do is try to enjoy being in bed and resting. This is irrespective of whether there is sleep or not. First, ensure that you direct your focus on how comfortable you are in bed and the manner in which your muscles are relaxed. In so doing, you are allowing your thoughts to drift slowly into sleep. In other words, you are allowing yourself be passive about sleep and your job is done! This way, sleep will come to you naturally.

Give yourself time to unwind before going to sleep

The best way you can achieve this is by ensuring that the last activity you are doing before going to bed is relatively passive. This means that you do not have to engage in activities that will require so much of your thoughts and trigger stress. Do not try to reflect on your life's problems or plan the week ahead among other unnecessary tasks that can be done gradually or at another time that is more convenient. The best you can do is to save such activities for the time when you feel fresh. Before you go to sleep, you can engage in activities such as; watching television, reading or talking. Unwind and let yourself go to sleep.

Employ a regular daytime cycle to allow you have nighttime sleep

The trick, in this case, is ensuring that you avoid taking naps during the day. Instead, you should employ the use of regular exercise that will induce fatigue and trigger normal sleep during nighttime. Minimize the intake of caffeine, alcohol or cigarette within several hours of retiring to bed. The best way in which you can establish a regular sleep pattern is by ensuring that you have a regular time for getting out of bed. Set your alarm clock to a reasonable time and ensure that you stick to it throughout the entire week. This way, you will be stabilizing your sleep easily.

Adjust sleep cycle prior to traveling

One of the things that have a great potential of disrupting sleep cycle is traveling across time zones, adjust your sleep cycle to match that of the new time zone. However, in cases where your travel is brief, stick to your regular schedule.

Avoid destructive activities

Control over illegal substance abuse

When it comes to things such as drugs and alcohol, these represent a great risk for people suffering from bipolar disorder. This is because, when you ingest these substances, you are impairing the activity of your medications. The main reason is that, when you engage in alcohol and drugs, you simply forget your condition and forget taking medications. This is also associated with increased rate of hospitalization. Particularly, stimulants are known to trigger episodes of mania and depression in people with bipolar disorder. Therefore, it is important that you assess your moods and the condition you are in before you make a decision to take alcohol or drugs.

This is the main reason why most bipolar treatments begin 30 days after one has been clean from drugs and alcohol. If it is about enjoying yourself, there are so many alternative events that you can engage in. Always ensure that you keep your doctor aware of any substances that you are using in the course of the treatment. Remember that you are the core member of your treatment group and thus, it is important that you keep the rest of the team up to date concerning your mood disorder.

How to get an accurate perspective on thoughts

Did you know that thought irrespective of whether they are true or not have a powerful effect on your mood? Well, this is the case and is the reason why it is important to have accurate thoughts. When one is suffering from a mood disorder, the truth is that they often suffer from the accuracy of thoughts. In depressive episodes of bipolar disorder, the thoughts are often negative in nature while in manic episodes, the thoughts are often positive.

It is important to come up with important strategies that will help you to avoid the effect of inaccurate thoughts. The best way in which you can prevent being pushed around by these inaccurate thoughts is treating them as hypotheses or guesses. This means that before you can accept the thought as true, it is important that you assess the thought to determine whether it is helpful or not. How can you assess your thoughts? You can assess your thoughts by ensuring that you look at the presence of evidence for and against each thought you have.

Ensure that you look at what alternative thoughts hold. The truth is that these alternative thoughts may actually have the accurate reflection of the reality. Your thoughts are often an influence of your present mood. Therefore, do not allow your mood to push you around into believing in things that are not accurate. Whenever you have challenges or difficulties in sorting out your thoughts, it might be very useful to discuss your thoughts with people that you trust. This could be a friend or a family member or even your therapist.

Suicidal thinking and self-care

As discussed earlier, it is evident that symptoms of bipolar disorder may include feeling hopeless. This is because when someone is experiencing intense symptoms of the mental illness, they often are very vulnerable to losing hope and feel that life is not worth living. It is these feelings that often slowly strip the mental patient of their sense of self-worth and soon they lose confidence and self-esteem. The consequences of these are, it allows thoughts of harming oneself to creep in and thus suicidal thoughts.

The truth about suicidal thoughts is that they can be frightening and overwhelming in most cases. This often takes place during both depressive and manic episodes of bipolar disorder. One important thing that you have to remember at all times is that suicidal thoughts and alteration of your behavior are all symptoms of bipolar disorder and just like other symptoms, they can be treated. Most of the people who have this illness often seek help and they are supported to get better. The first step, in this case, is for the patient and their family to be aware of the signs of suicide so that they can look out for these.

Some of these warning signs may include; frequent talks about committing suicide or thoughts about death. In other cases, the person might be making concerning comments about being hopeless and worthless indicating that they have lost their self-esteem and confidence and this could potentially pose a great threat to them. Some of the statements that they could be making are; "It would be better if I just died", or "I want out". Other indicators may be that the patient is in a worse situation of depression and experiences sudden changes in their moods. They could voluntarily expose themselves to things that might harm them. Finally, the patient may also be trying to sort their affairs in certain order such as talking about their will, finances and ensuring that all this are patched up in case they die.

 If these warning signs are evident, it is important that you take the relevant and necessary steps to protect yourself and your loved ones. The best way you can do this is by simply taking the discussion up with the doctor. You have to understand that suicidal thoughts are symptoms and this is the very reason why you should report this to a mental health professional so that the necessary help can be administered. Based on how severe these thoughts are, it is important during this time, to ensure that you or your loved one accept a brief hospital stay for close monitoring. The purpose of the hospital stay is not to burden you or strip you of your freedom. Instead, it is important in offering you the help, support, and protection that you need until you are feeling better. As a matter of fact, this is the most fundamental and critical aspects of care. A person requires protection during this time of severe symptoms so that they have all the chances and opportunities of improving. I, therefore, want you to take every step necessary to ensure that you are protected and make good use of your treatment team for your own good.

One of the straightforward strategies you can employ is making the process of getting help very easy. This is one of the techniques which have been shown by research to play a significant role in enhancing safety in situations where one has suicidal thoughts. The very step of ensuring that the person has relevant contact information has been demonstrated to play a significant role in protecting individuals from suicidal action. Therefore, my request to you is to create a contact information on an index card and share this card with people who care about you. Store an extra card in a place where one can easily have access to it, such as; the kitchen cabinets, at the very front of your phonebook, drawers or on your refrigerator. On the card, ensure that you clearly and correctly record the numbers of your healthcare providers, local emergency room as well as the admission personnel in the hospital who can get you quick help.

At all times, when it comes to minimizing risks, it is important to always include a suicide prevention plan together with your treatment contract. In this case, it is advisable that you work with your doctor and support team to integrate important planning component in the contract. The main reason for this is so that each person involved is aware of the warning signs that they are supposed to watch out for as well as the actions to take if they feel that you are slipping into suicidal thoughts.

Additionally, it is important for you as a bipolar disorder patient, together with your family, to be aware of the things that you should do in case of an emergency. This includes calling your doctor or making emergency arrangements with caregivers the moment you feel suicidal. Also, you can seek help from a trusted friend or family member to guard you to safety until you can get the help that you need. You can also contact emergency services whenever you think that you cannot control the feeling of harming yourself, you are hearing voices or you feel that you really want to commit suicide.

How your family can help

Your family is your support system. They play a crucial role in helping you to cope with the bipolar disorder and its symptoms. I encourage you and your family to ensure that you read this book back to back. It is especially of great importance that you review the content presented in this chapter together with your family.

The first thing that I would like you to do is to think of your family as a critical part of your treatment team. This means that you have to make a decision with them on how they can offer you their care. Ensure that they fully understand the essence of your psychiatric care. To get the best support is through effective communication between you, your family and the support team on a whole. Every single mentor and member of your support team must be on one accord to be able to accomplish effective results. It is especially crucial that all persons involved, have the same goal, which evidently, is to get you better.

Understand that when you improve communication, you are simply ensuring that you are lowering the chances of stress at home and thus boosting your relationship with your family. A tolerant and low key surrounding at home is the recipe for minimizing depressive and manic episodes of bipolar disorder. The truth is, maintaining a low atmosphere like I previously mentioned is quite challenging. It is evident that most families find it very difficult to address emotionally charged issues. This is the main reason why so many bipolar patients complain that every strong emotion they experience is attributed to their mental illness rather than what they really feel as a person. On the other hand, family members complain that the person is over-reactive about small issues and take everything to a highly emotional level. It is also a frustrating situation when most members of the support team try to evade every topic that is brought forth for discussion because they have the mindset that this is too intense for you.

A very useful and practical technique that you can employ in this case is the whisper rule. This is one of the techniques that requires the use of a simple agreement where, whenever one feels that the topic of discussion is getting supercharged, it is recommended and allowed for them to request for the discussion to be held in a whisper. However, in case this whisper rule is violated, the discussion is put out for a given period of time like 2-3 hours. In most cases, you will realize that patients who employ the use of this method in their support team often instruct their families to abide by the whisper rule to indicate that the state of their mood is normal. Additionally, the times when they fail to adhere to the whisper rule is an indication of illness.

Communication Skills

Have you ever heard of a gardener's tip? Well, when you are having a discussion with your treatment team, it pays to employ the use of this tip. The tip states that "*It pays to water the flowers, not the weeds*". This gardener's tip emphasizes the importance of focusing attention on what is working in the relationship and not the things that are going wrong. This means that if you want your relationship with the family and the treatment team to yield fruit, you have to ensure that the entire team is aware that you want them to do things that make you happy. Some of these things include ensuring that they remain considerate to your illness and they help at home among others. In most cases, it is quite sad that many people only pay attention to the things that are negative. They will complain about the things that are not working. It is this negative attention in most cases increase bad feelings and thus impairing with the effort to address an existing problem.

Another significant thing is that paying attention to addressing the problem is of uttermost importance when it comes to bipolar disorder patients. Problems have to be addressed once and for all. The people with bipolar disorder often do not appreciate negative feedback, as this only worsen their moods rather than help with the issues at hand. This means that effective modes of communication have to be employed.

When it comes to offering approvals to other people, family members are often inclined to giving approval to others. It is important that you use this power here! It is very critical to ensure that you appreciate the bipolar patient for the effort towards recovery by letting them know that they are on track. This is simply by giving verbal feedback, positive intonation, pleasant and appreciative eye contact, a hug, kiss, and touch among others. These are the most important strategies that you can employ to ensure that you communicate effectively and support the patient through their illness, this will be of great significance to the reduction of negative emotions.

Effective listening skills

All too often, arguments and bad attitudes arise in the family. This is frequently because of misunderstandings that revolve around what was said. The main reason for this is because each party in the conversation fails to pay attention to what the other person is saying and thus jumps into conclusions. This is what causes an emotional escalation, feelings of anger, hopelessness, and frustrations. In order to ensure that you prevent this from taking place, it is significant that each party involved in the conversation communicate with a high degree of clarity. This means that you have to get feedback to the previous message before you can communicate the second message.

Effective listening is a skill which requires that you pay attention to what is being said so that you get the accurate information from the other party. When you do this, you will simply communicate accurately to the speaker indicating in your response that you heard them loud and clear. This is what effective listening and communication skill requires. To be able to achieve this, it is important that you keep your skills and counter arguments in check long enough to ensure that you are devoted to getting the message accurately. Your role is not to give a quick response to everything that is being said. Instead, it is your responsibility to demonstrate to the person that is speaking that you heard and comprehend what they said. Once you have received the message clearly, only then can you consider giving a feedback to the message.

Some of the steps that will help you to ensure that you are effectively listening to the message that the person is trying to put across to you include the following; Giving the speaker a clear signal that you are attentive to what they are saying. The best way you can do this is simply maintaining close eye contact and nodding at every point they make. Secondly, you can ask questions in the middle of communication. This is to make the points that are being communicated clear to you. The main goal is not to debate what is being said. Rather, it is to understand where the speaker is coming from with their argument. Thirdly, you can repeat what the speaker said back to him or her so that you can verify if what was said, was indeed what you interpreted. If the speaker is not in agreement with that, it is not important to debate what they said. The most important thing, in this case, is to have them make clarification concerning what they meant. Once both you and the speaker are in agreement with the message, then it is your turn to give a response.

Chapter Five: Stories of Coping and Courage

These are some of the stories that members of my support group have made the decision to share with you so that you can enhance your understanding of what feelings one has when they are diagnosed with a mood disorder. This also helps you to determine what treatment options are available, the manner in which you can deal with matters that surround your relationships, career and social life. This also includes what has worked for them while coping with their mental illnesses. The main theme in this chapter is to ensure that you and I fight social stigma that has been at the forefront of preventing people from seeking help. The importance of this is coming to the realization that there is hope in recovery irrespective of what circumstances stand in the way.

In spite of the fact that each story, in this case, is different and unique in their own way, the truth is that they all resonate around the same themes. These themes are;

Hope- they all have a strong belief that they will soon get well.

Support- they all have sought help from a wide range of sources. These sources include, but is not limited to, therapists, doctors, families, friends, support groups among others.

Determination- they continue seeking the best treatment they can get. This is evident through the kind of dedication they have to improve their health conditions.

Commitment- they all have demonstrated commitment by sticking to their treatment plans despite the challenges that they have faced and the relapses associated with some medications.

Before we can delve into what each bipolar disorder patient has to say about their journey, it is important to note that depression and mania in bipolar patients do not translate into weakness and being flawed. Rather, we have to understand that this illness affects over 20 million people across the globe. With the correct form of treatment, it is possible to manage the symptoms associated with the disorder without necessarily interfering with your life. When you seek treatment for your mental illness, it does not mean that you have failed in any way. It only means that you are strong enough and have the self-courage and sense of feeling better.

The stories here are of different patients at different stages of their illnesses and wellness. The one thing to remember is that it often takes different time frames before a correct diagnosis is made or even before right treatment is found for you. Some have had to try a wide range of methods or even be patient until their treatment is effective. Despite the fact that this is very challenging, the most important thing is holding on to faith and be optimistic that things will work out. If you are suffering from the same condition as the rest of us, do not give up. The key to your recovery is keeping the right mindset, be persistent in your search for the right treatment and the right support from the people around you.

1. *Mercy*

Mercy is a young lady who has struggled with bipolar disorder for a very long time without knowing it. What stands out for her is the fact that she has struggled with depression since her early childhood. This is highlighted by the fact that she did not want to take medication. She noted, that despite the fact that her doctors prescribed medications, she just wouldn't take them. However, along the journey, she had to accept her condition and begin taking medications for the sake of her daughter. At the very beginning, antidepressants seemed promising in managing her depression until the time when she became manic and had to be hospitalized. After many years of suffering, she finally received the correct diagnosis of bipolar disorder and received the treatment she needed.

What worked? - The correct diagnosis that caused the doctor to prescribe mood stabilizers and antipsychotics. Additionally, her medication was even made effective by simply getting support from her daughter, family, friends and her church. Through this, she and her daughter have learned so much about bipolar disorders. Though she might have drifted a little due to stress, she continues to work closely with her doctors to make her treatment plan effective.

2. *Matthew, 19 years*

Matthew has been in and out of the hospital for a very long time. Just a few months ago, he had a major manic episode while in college. At the time, he was using drugs with his friends before he felt a sudden impulse came over him. This was not the effects of the drugs they had been using because the effect had already worn out. As he recalls, the day after, he felt as though he was on top of the world and owned everything in the universe. He felt as though spending time sleeping was a great waste of time and so he stayed up all night reading and writing poems, a gift he did not know he had. He then spent the following day shopping around for luxurious items such as clothes, shoes, food and treating friends to lunch and dinner. Coming home, Matthew's mother noticed that he was manic because his sister is also bipolar. This is when he was taken to the hospital.

What has worked? - Well, according to Matthew, things are always in place as long as he is on medication. At first, he was afraid that the medication would change his personality and this is the reason why he was still living in denial about him having a mental illness. Matthew was hospitalized a number of times for discontinuing his medications, he hated the hospital but he had to keep taking his meds in order to get well. Additionally, whenever he had manic episodes, he would say stuff he could not take back, and this he said, cost him two girlfriends and thus, he resorted to taking medications.

With the help of family, doctors and a sister who is bipolar too, Matthew has managed well. Additionally, he joined a foundation for bipolar patients which has been very beneficial in helping him cope through the acceptance phase. Now, he has a support treatment team that helps him to stay away from drugs and thus stabilizing his medication and moods.

3. *Yolanda, age 44*

Yolanda was adopted from an orphanage in Japan when she was a year and a half old. She was so much neglected in the orphanage and because of this, she was suffering from stunted growth and had challenges walking. According to her, the trauma of her childhood was the main contributing factor to her depression. She narrates a story of when she was a child and wrote in her journals that she died of malaria. The main reason for this is her hopelessness that made her believe she was not going to last beyond a certain age. After the birth of her second child, she fell into the worst depression ever! Whenever her baby cried in the crib, she would be in agony and anguish. She would remember her childhood as an orphan. She would get upset and became harmful to herself. Five years later, she became suicidal and was hospitalized. It was this time that she received a correct diagnosis for bipolar disorder.

What has worked? - She says that she has to adhere to medications. Her close working relationship with her doctor has been very beneficial in making relevant adjustments in her medications to reduce the side effects while ensuring that depression is controlled. Her regular contact with friends has been very instrumental in supporting her through treatment and mood stability. She now enjoys motherhood and enjoys engaging in recreational activities such as; playing the piano and guitar for relaxation. When she is depressed, she is reminded by her support team of her positive traits and the love of her children.

4. *Mark, age 67*

He was first diagnosed with bipolar disorder in 1980. However, he threw away all his medications because he had not come to terms with the fact that he was indeed bipolar. While on a business trip, he had a manic episode. He thought that he could develop wings and fly. When he got home, his family wanted him hospitalized. He stayed in the hospital for three days and spent that time praying. Mark hoped that once he was released from the hospital, he would never have to suffer from the illness anymore. This is when he joined DBSA group in California where they worked together with his wife to get more groups started to support people like him.

What has worked? – According to Mark, once he accepted that he was having a problem, it served as the key to getting the help that he needed. He says that he surrounded himself with people who had bipolar disorder and sharing their experiences has extremely helped in his recovery process. By joining a support group he has changed his life. He continues to inspire people today by motivating and encouraging them that they can get better. He is determined to employ any method he can to tell his story to the world so that they can get the healing they need whether people agree with it or not.

5. _Jane, age 52_

As a freshman in college several years ago, Jane first experienced depressive episodes that adversely affected her performance in school and this caused her to leave school for a year. After her graduation, she had another severe episode of depression that made her suicidal. She would drive around town looking for somewhere she could purchase a gun from. This is the point where she realized that she needed help and she sought for it. Jane was diagnosed with depression and she was put on psychotherapy. However, even so, she was not getting proper treatment because all the treatment was aiming at was to fix her sexual orientation. One night, she did not have sleep and kept thinking of how to restructure certain psychiatric theories and sharing this with her doctor, she was diagnosed with bipolar disorder.

What has worked? – The fact that she herself is a trained professional psychiatrist. Therefore, she knows that mood disorder does not last forever and thus playing a key role in helping her cope with her mental illness. She is also well aware of the many drugs on the market that come up each day aiming to improve her condition. This is the thing which drives her to try them and hang on to the hope that she can get better. Her strong spiritual belief in God has helped her so much in asking God to grant her serenity to accept the things that she cannot change. Her partner also offers incredible support to make her constantly aware that she is not a failure.

6. *Ricardo, age 60*

It was 1979 that Ric experienced the worst depressive episodes of his life. Unfortunately, in

1980, he had another severe manic episode. While in New York, he spent a long period of time seeking the right treatment but it never came through. This is when he and the wife decided that the best thing to do was to learn from people who were suffering from the same disease and how they were coping with their conditions. They started a group in 1981 which has since grown into a whole institution that supports bipolar patients.

What has worked? – He says that one of the things he is grateful about is the fact that he has been free from bipolar episodes for over 20 years. This, he says is due to excellent treatment by his psychopharmacologist, a supportive wife, dedicated work with a psychologist and his work for the community of people living with bipolar disorder. He admits that the greatest challenge is that of self-stigma, guilt and being a hypochondriac. However, working closely with support teams has enabled him to win back his confidence and appreciate his leadership skills.

7. Jennifer, age 45

Over the years, it is really sad to hear that Jennifer grew up to have tantrums and tendency to cry for no reason whatsoever. She says that she would sometimes break every glass in her house. The main reason for this is that she would anger over small things and destroy everything, then go to bed and feel at peace. She then decided to find treatment from a doctor. However, her family discouraged her telling her that medication was bad, the doctors around were unqualified, and that only if she had faith, she would get well. She heeded to their advice and tried to take control of her episodes by herself. However, as years went by, her situation was getting worse and she decided to get help. She tried several doctors and finally got one who gave her the right prescription.

What has worked? – According to her, the support she gets from her husband is priceless. This is because he helps her stay up to date with information that revolves around bipolar disorder. He also ensures that she never stops her medication and whenever she is not well, he would be the one that supports her and takes care of the home and do the house chores. They often talk about their feelings freely so that they do not end up resenting each other. Working with her doctor is another contributing factor to her getting better. With her doctor, she is able to keep a diary that helps her keep track of her moods which helps in tracking her progress.

Conclusion

From the information that we have covered in this book, it is evident that there is not yet a cure for bipolar disorder. The strong possibility is the fact that if you are diagnosed with bipolar disorder, you certainly require long-term medication and support on a continuous basis. The main aim of this is to ensure that you have the ability to sustainably combat the potentially harmful nature of the illness. However, based on the many accounts that we have covered in this book, the most frightening moment in your life after your diagnosis is the ability to accept your condition. Once you have done this, the many information and tips covered in this book have paved the way for you to live a normal and successful life without fear of stigma, ridicule, or shame. After you have confronted the symptoms of your illness, create your novel experience and strive towards your goals with a positive attitude and a greater personal insight. It is with this insight that we get the right professional mental health and support.

While bipolar disorder is often associated with mood changes, It is important that you understand that these moods are distinct from the ordinary mood swings. First, this is because of the intensity differences. The reason for this is that mood swings associated with bipolar disorder are often severe. The second difference is the length of time in which the mood swings last. When one is suffering from mood disorder associated with mania or depression, it can last for weeks, months or even a year. However, if it is the rapid cycling of bipolar disorder, it may take a short time but is characterized by a sudden shift from one extreme to another. Lastly, it often causes a significant life interference. This extreme in mood often result in serious problems that could be interpersonal, career related or even worse, detrimental to personal growth and survival.

It is therefore evident that bipolar disorder is a complex disorder for any psychiatrist to manage. The main reason for this is based on the fact that it is associated with the complex occurrence of episodes as well as comorbid disorders. Comorbid Disorder is the combination or presence of two or more chronic diseases or conditions existing in a patient at the same time. Additionally, lack of patients' ability to adhere to treatments makes the problem much more challenging to manage effectively. It then poses a great public health risk because of the high rates or mortality and morbidity among the patients. Some of the factors that make treatment plans complex are the fluctuation in mood episodes. Additionally, treatment is compounded by the impact that the episodes have on the wellbeing of the patient, failure to take medications as required as well as comorbid psychiatric disorders as mentioned earlier. This is the very reason why guidelines have been put in place to manage mania, depression, and other bipolar disorder episodes. The good thing is that additional treatments are still being developed. This ensures that the future is well taken care of.

Considering the fact that bipolar disorder is a lifelong illness. It is characterized as far-reaching and often devastating symptoms that affect both the life of the afflicted and that of the caregiver. Nonetheless, increased research on the various aspects that underlie the illness promises to offer an in-depth understanding of what really causes the disease. This information is very fundamental in forming the basis for better understanding of the manner in which the burdens of the disease has on patients and caregivers and can be significantly reduced. It is through such efforts as psychosocial support, customer and advocacy movements among others support groups that will actively champion the eradication of the illness from the future generation.

Thank you for reading this book on Bipolar Disorder. I sincerely hope that the information in this book has equipped you with the necessary tools needed to combat your condition or that of your loved one so you may lead a happy, positive and healthy lifestyle. good luck.

Other books by Author

Sociapath and Psychopath-How to detect, avoid, and counter attack their behavior

Breaking The Chains of a Pschopath and Sociapath: Learning how to live Again